D1038454

the First
Christmas Tree
and Other Stories

HENRY VAN DYKE

the First
Christmas Tree

and Other Stories

Mildly Modernized

PARACLETE PRESS
BREWSTER, MASSACHUSETTS

The First Christmas Tree and Other Stories

2011 First Printing This Edition
2002 First Printing Original Paraclete Press Edition

Modernized text copyright © 2002 by Paraclete Press, Inc.

ISBN 978-1-55725-983-7

Original edition of *The First Christmas Tree*
© 1907 by Charles Scribner's Sons.
Original edition of *The Spirit of Christmas*
© 1905, 1957 by Charles Scribner's Sons.

Scripture quotations are taken from the Revised Standard Version of the Bible, © 1946, 1952, 1971 by the Division of Christian Education of the National Council of the Churches of Christ in the USA. Used by permission.

The Library of Congress has catalogued the original
Paraclete Press edition of this book as follows:

Van Dyke, Henry, 1852-1933.
    The first Christmas tree and other stories : mildly modernized /by Henry Van Dyke.
        p. cm.
    First work originally published: The first Christmas tree. New York : C. Scribner's Sons, 1906. 2nd work originally published: The spirit of Christmas. New York : C. Scribner's Sons, 1905.
        ISBN 1-55725-315-3 (hardcover)
        I. Christmas. 2. Christmas–Prayer-books and devotions–English. I. Van Dyke, Henry, 1852-1933. First Christmas tree. II. Van Dyke, Henry, 1852-1933. Spirit of Christmas. III. Title.
    BV45.V3 2002
    242'.335–dc2i
                                                                2002008364

10 9 8 7 6 5 4 3 2 1

All rights reserved. No portion of this book may be reproduced, stored in a retrieval system, or transmitted in any form or by any means—electronic, mechanical, photocopy, recording, or any other—except for brief quotations in printed reviews, without the prior permission of the publisher.

Published by Paraclete Press
Brewster, Massachusetts
www.paracletepress.com

Printed in the United States of America

CONTENTS

Keeping Christmas

He who observes the day,
Observes it in honor of the Lord.

ROMANS 14:6

I T IS A GOOD THING TO OBSERVE CHRISTMAS DAY. The mere marking of times and seasons, when all agree to stop work and make merry together, is a wise and wholesome custom. It helps us to feel the supremacy of the common life over the individual life. It reminds us to set our own little watch, now and then, by the great clock of humanity that runs on sun time.

But there is a better thing than the observance of Christmas day, and that is keeping Christmas.

Are you willing to forget what you have done for other people, and to remember what other people have done for you; to ignore what the world owes you, and to think what you owe the world; to put your rights in the background, and your duties in the middle distance, and your chances to do a little more than your duty in the foreground; to see that your fellows are just as real as you are, and try to look behind their faces to their hearts, hungry for joy; to admit that probably the only good reason for your existence is not what you are going to get out of life, but what you are going to give to life; to close your book of complaints against the management of the universe, and look around you for a place where you can sow a few seeds of happiness—are you willing to do these things even for a day? Then you can keep Christmas.

Are you willing to stoop down and consider the needs and the desires of little children; to remember the weakness and loneliness of people who are growing old; to stop asking how much your friends love you, and ask yourself whether you love them enough; to bear in mind the things that other people have to bear on their hearts; to try to understand what those who live in the same house with you really want, without waiting for them to tell you; to trim your lamp so that it will give more light and less smoke, and to carry it in front so that your shadow will fall behind you; to make a grave for your ugly thoughts, and a garden for your kindly feelings, with the gate open—are you willing to do these things even for a day? Then you can keep Christmas.

Are you willing to believe that love is the strongest thing in the world—stronger than hate, stronger than evil, stronger than death—and that the blessed life that began in Bethlehem two thousand years ago is the image and brightness of the Eternal Love? Then you can keep Christmas.

And if you keep it for a day, why not always?

But you can never keep it alone.

the First Christmas Tree

I

THE CALL OF THE WOODSMAN

The Day Before Christmas, in the Year of Our Lord 722.

BROAD SNOW-MEADOWS GLISTENED WHITE along the banks of the river Moselle; pallid hillsides bloomed with mystic roses where the glow of the setting sun still lingered upon them; an arch of clearest, faintest azure bent overhead; in the center of the aerial landscape rose the massive walls of the cloister of Pfalzel, gray to the east, purple to the west; silence over all—a gentle, eager, conscious stillness, diffused through the air like perfume, as if earth and sky were hushing themselves to hear the voice of the river faintly murmuring down the valley.

In the cloister, too, there was silence at the sunset hour. All day long there had been a strange and joyful stir among the nuns. A breeze of curiosity and excitement had swept along the corridors and through every quiet cell.

The elder sisters—the provost, the deaconess, the stewardess, the portress with her huge bunch of keys jingling at her waist—had been hurrying to and fro, busied with household cares. In the huge kitchen there was a bustle of hospitable preparation. The little bandy-legged dogs that kept the spits turning before the fires had been trotting steadily for many an hour until their tongues hung out for want of breath. The big black pots swinging from the cranes had bubbled and gurgled and shaken and sent out puffs of appetizing steam.

Lazarus and Mary's sister, Martha, was in her element. It was a field day for her virtues.

The younger sisters, the pupils of the convent, had forsaken their Latin books and their embroidery frames, their manuscripts and their miniatures, and fluttered through the halls in little flocks like merry snowbirds, all in black and white, chattering and whispering together. This was no day for tedious task work, no day for grammar or arithmetic, no day for picking out illuminated letters in red and gold on stiff parchment or patiently chasing intricate patterns over thick cloth with the slow needle. It was a holiday. A famous visitor had come to the convent.

It was Winfried of England, whose name in the Roman tongue was Boniface, and whom men called the Apostle of Germany. A great preacher, a wonderful scholar, he had written a Latin grammar himself—think of it—and he could hardly sleep without a book under his pillow. But, more than all, he was a great and daring traveler, a venturesome pilgrim, a high priest of romance.

He had left his home and his fair estate in Wessex; he would not stay in the rich monastery of Nutescelle, even though they had chosen him as the abbot; he had refused a bishopric at the court of King Karl. Nothing would content him but to go out into the wild woods and preach to the heathen.

Up and down through the forests of Hesse and Thuringia and along the borders of Saxony he had wandered for years, with a handful of companions, sleeping under the trees, crossing mountains and marshes, now here, now there, never satisfied with ease and comfort, always in love with hardship and danger.

What a man he was! Fair and slight, but straight as a spear and strong as an oaken staff. His face was still young, its smooth skin bronzed by wind and sun. His gray eyes, clear and kind, flashed like fire when he spoke of his adventures and of the evil deeds of the false priests with whom he contended.

What tales he had told that day! Not of miracles wrought by sacred relics, not of courts and councils and splendid cathedrals, though he knew much of these things and had been to Rome and had received the Pope's blessing. No, today he had spoken of long journeys by sea and land, of perils by fire and flood, of wolves and bears and fierce snowstorms and black nights in the lonely forest, of dark altars of heathen gods, and strange, bloody sacrifices and narrow escapes from murderous bands of wandering savages.

The little novices had gathered around him, and their faces had grown pale and their eyes bright as they listened with parted lips, entranced in admiration, twining their arms about one another's shoulders and holding closely together, half in fear, half in delight. The older nuns had turned from their tasks and paused, in passing by, to hear the pilgrim's story. Too well they knew the truth of what he spoke. Many a one among them had seen the smoke rising from the ruins of her father's roof. Many a one had a brother far away in the wild country to whom her heart went out night and day, wondering if he were still among the living.

But now the excitements of that wonderful day were over; the hour of the evening meal had come; the inmates of the cloister were assembled in the refectory.

On the dais sat the stately Abbess Addula, daughter of King Dagobert, looking a princess indeed in her violet tunic, with the hood and cuffs of her long white robe trimmed with fur and a snowy veil resting like a crown on her snowy hair. At her right hand was the honored guest and at her left hand her grandson, the young Prince Gregor, a big, manly boy, just returned from studies away from home.

The long, shadowy hall, with its dark brown rafters and beams; the double rows of nuns, with their pure veils and fair faces; the ruddy glow of the slanting sunbeams striking upwards through the tops of the windows and painting a pink glow high up on the walls—it was all as beautiful as a picture, and as silent. For this was the rule of the cloister, that at the table all should sit in stillness for a little while, and then one should read aloud while the rest listened.

"It is my grandson's turn to read today," said the abbess to Winfried. "We shall see how much he has learned in the school. Read, Gregor; the place in the book is marked."

The tall lad rose from his seat and turned the pages of the manuscript. It was a copy of Jerome's version of the Scriptures in Latin, and the marked place was in the letter of Saint Paul to the Ephesians, the passage where he describes the preparation of the Christian as the arming of a warrior for glorious battle. The young voice rang out clearly, rolling the sonorous words, without slip or stumbling, to the end of the chapter.

Winfried listened, smiling. "My son," he said as the reader paused, "that was bravely read. Do you understand what you have read?"

"Surely, father," answered the boy. "It was taught me by the masters at Treves, and we have read this epistle clear through, from beginning to end, so that I almost know it by heart."

Then he began again to repeat the passage, turning away from the page as if to show his skill.

But Winfried stopped him with a friendly lifting of the hand.

"Not so, my son; that was not my meaning. When we pray, we speak to God; when we read, it is God who speaks to us. I ask whether you have heard what he has said to you, in your own words, in the common speech. Come, give us again the message of the warrior and his armor and his battle, in the mother tongue, so that all can understand it."

The boy hesitated, blushed, stammered; then he came around to Winfried's seat, bringing the book. "Take the book, father," he cried, "and read it for me. I cannot see the meaning plainly, though I love the sound of the words. Religion I know, and the doctrines of our faith, and the life of priests and nuns in the cloister, for which my grandmother designs me, though it suits me little. And fighting I know, and the life of warriors and heroes, for I have read of it in Virgil and the ancients, and heard a bit from the soldiers at Treves; and I wish to taste more of it, for it suits me much. But how the two lives fit together, or what need there is of armor for a clerk in holy orders, I can never see. Tell me the meaning, for if there is one in all the world who knows it, I am sure it is none other than you."

So Winfried took the book and closed it, clasping the boy's hand with his own.

"Let us first dismiss the others to their vespers," said he, "so that they will not become weary."

A sign from the abbess, a chanted benediction, a murmuring of sweet voices, and a soft rustling of many feet over the rushes on the floor: the gentle tide of noise flowed out through the doors and ebbed away down the corridors. The three at the head of the table were left alone in the darkening room.

Then Winfried began to translate the parable of the soldier into the realities of life.

At every turn he knew how to flash a new light into the picture out of his own experience. He spoke of combat with self, and of wrestling with dark spirits in solitude. He spoke of the demons that men had worshiped for centuries in the wilderness, and whose malice they invoked against the stranger who ventured into the gloomy forest. Gods, they called them, and told strange tales of their dwelling among the impenetrable branches of the oldest trees and in the caverns of the shaggy hills, of their riding on the wind horse and hurling spears of lightning against their foes. Gods they were not, but foul spirits of the air, rulers of the darkness. Was there not glory and honor in fighting with them, in daring their anger under the shield of faith, in putting them to flight with the sword of truth? What better adventure could a brave man ask than to go forth against them and wrestle with them and conquer them?

"Look, my friends," said Winfried, "how sweet and peaceful is this convent tonight, on the eve of the nativity of the Prince of Peace! It is a garden full of flowers in the heart of winter, a nest among the branches of a great tree shaken by the winds, a still haven on the edge of a tempestuous sea. And this is what religion means for those who are chosen and called to quiet and prayer and meditation.

"But out there in the wide forest, who knows what storms are raging tonight in the hearts of mankind, though all the woods are still? Who knows what haunts of wrath and cruelty and fear are closed tonight against the advent of the Prince of Peace? And shall I tell you what religion means to those who are called and chosen to dare and to fight and to conquer the world for Christ? It means to launch out into the deep. It means to go against the strongholds of the adversary. It means to struggle to win an entrance for their Master everywhere. What helmet is strong enough for this strife except the helmet of salvation? What breastplate can guard a man against these fiery darts but the breastplate of righteousness? What shoes can stand the wear of these journeys but the preparation of the gospel of peace?"

"Shoes?" he cried again, and laughed as if a sudden thought had struck him. He thrust out his foot, covered with a heavy cowhide boot, laced high about his leg with thongs of skin.

"See here what shoes are worn by a fighting man of the cross! I have seen the boots of the Bishop of Tours: white kid, broidered with silk; a day in the bogs would tear them to shreds. I have seen the sandals that the monks use on the high-roads—yes, and worn them: Ten pairs of them I have worn out and thrown away in a single journey. Now I wear shoes made of the tough-est hides, hard as iron; no rock can cut them, no branch can tear them. Yet I have outworn more than one pair of these, and I shall outwear many more before my journeys are ended. And I think, if God is gracious to me, that I shall die wearing them. Better that than in a soft bed with silk coverings. The boots of a warrior, a hunter, a woodsman—these are my preparation of the gospel of peace."

"Come, Gregor," he said, laying his brown hand on the youth's shoulder, "come, wear the forester's boots with me. This is the life to which we are called. Be strong in the Lord, a hunter of the demons, a subduer of the wilderness, a woodsman of the faith. Come!"

The boy's eyes sparkled. He turned to his grandmother. She shook her head vigorously.

"No, father," she said, "do not draw the lad away from my side with these wild words. I need him to help me with my labors, to cheer my old age."

"Do you need him more than the Master does?" asked Winfried. "And will you take the wood that is fit for a bow to make a woman's spinning staff?"

"But I fear for the child. Your life is too hard for him. He will perish with hunger in the woods."

"Once," said Winfried, smiling, "we were camped by the bank of the river Ohru. The table was spread for the morning meal, but my comrades cried that it was empty: The provisions were exhausted. We must go without breakfast and perhaps starve before we could escape from the wilderness. While they complained, a fish hawk flew up from the river with flapping wings and let fall a great pike in the midst of the camp. There was food enough and to spare. Never have I seen the righteous forsaken, or his offspring begging bread."

"But the fierce pagans of the forest," cried the abbess—"they may pierce the boy with their arrows, or dash out his brains with their axes. He is only a child, too young for the dangers of strife."

"A child in years," replied Winfried, "but a man in spirit. And if the hero must fall early in the battle, he wears the brighter crown, not a withered leaf, not a fallen flower."

The aged princess trembled a little. She drew Gregor close to her side, and laid her hand gently on his brown hair.

"I am not sure that he wants to leave me yet. Besides, there is no horse in the stable to give him now, and he cannot go as befits the grandson of a king."

Gregor looked straight into her eyes.

"Grandmother," said he, "dear grandmother, if you will not give me a horse to ride with this man of God, I will go with him on foot."

II

THE TRAIL THROUGH
THE FOREST

WO YEARS HAD PASSED, TO A DAY, ALMOST TO
an hour, since that Christmas Eve in the
cloister of Pfalzel. A little company of pilgrims,
fewer than twenty men, was creeping slowly
northward through the wide forest that
rolled over the hills of central Germany.

At the head of the band marched Winfried, clad
in a tunic of fur, with his long black robe belted
high about his waist so that it might not hinder
his stride. His hunter's boots were crusted with
snow. Drops of ice sparkled like jewels along the

23

thongs that bound his legs. There was no other ornament to his dress except the bishop's cross hanging on his breast and the broad silver clasp that fastened his cloak about his neck. He carried a strong, tall staff in his hand, fashioned at the top into the form of a cross.

Close beside him, keeping step like a familiar comrade, was the young Prince Gregor. Long marches through the wilderness had stretched his limbs and broadened his back and made a man of him in stature as well as in spirit. His jacket and cap were of wolf skin, and on his shoulder he carried an axe with a broad, shining blade. He was a mighty woodsman now and could make a spray of chips fly around him as he hewed his way through the trunk of a spruce tree. Behind these leaders followed a pair of teamsters, guiding a crude sled loaded with food and the equipage of the camp and drawn by two big, shaggy horses blowing thick clouds of steam from their frosty nostrils. Tiny icicles hung from the hairs on their lips. Their flanks were smoking. They sank above the fetlocks at every step in the soft snow.

Last of all came the rear guard, armed with bows and javelins. It was no child's play in those days to cross Europe on foot.

The eerie woodland, somber and limitless, covered hill and valley, tableland and mountain peak. There were wide moors where the wolves hunted in packs as if the devil drove them, and tangled thickets where the lynx and the boar made their lairs. Fierce bears lurked among the rocky passes and had not yet learned to fear the face of humans. The gloomy recesses of the forest gave shelter to inhabitants who were still more cruel and dangerous than beasts of prey—outlaws and sturdy robbers and madmen and bands of wandering pillagers.

The pilgrim who would pass from the mouth of the Tiber to the mouth of the Rhine must travel with a little army of bodyguards, or else trust in God and keep his arrows loose in the quiver.

The travelers were surrounded by an ocean of trees, so vast, so full of endless billows, that it seemed to be pressing on every side to overwhelm them. Gnarled oaks, with branches twisted and knotted as if in rage, rose in groves like tidal waves. Smooth forests of beech trees, round and gray, swept over the knolls and slopes of land in a mighty ground swell. But most of all, the multitude of pines and firs, innumerable and monotonous, with straight, stark trunks and branches woven together in an unbroken flood of darkest green, crowded through the valleys and over the hills, rising on the highest ridges into ragged crests like the foaming edge of sea breakers.

Through this sea of shadows ran a narrow stream of shining whiteness: an ancient Roman road, covered with snow. It was as if some great ship had ploughed through the green ocean long ago and left behind it a thick, smooth wake of foam. Along this open track the travelers held their way—heavily, for the drifts were deep; warily, for the hard winter had driven many packs of wolves down from the moors.

The pilgrims' steps were noiseless, but the sleds creaked over the dry snow, and the horses' panting throbbed through the still, cold air. The pale blue shadows on the western side of the road grew longer. The sun, declining through its shallow arch, dropped behind the treetops. Darkness followed swiftly, as if it had been a bird of prey waiting for this sign to swoop down upon the world.

"Father," said Gregor to the leader, "surely this day's march is done. It is time to rest, and eat, and sleep. If we press onward now, we cannot see our steps; and will not that be against the word of the psalmist David, who bids us not to put confidence in the legs of a man?"

Winfried laughed. "No, my son Gregor," he said, "you have tripped, even now, upon your text. For David said only, 'I take no pleasure in the legs of a man.' And so say I, for I am not minded to spare your legs or mine until we go farther on our way and do what must be done this night. Draw your belt tighter, my son, and hew away this tree that has fallen across the road, for our camp ground is not here."

The youth obeyed; two of the foresters sprang to help him. And while the soft fir wood yielded to the stroke of the axes and the snow flew from the bending branches, Winfried turned and spoke to his followers in a cheerful voice that refreshed them like wine.

"Courage, brothers, and forward yet a little. The moon will light us shortly, and the path is plain. I know well that the journey is weary, and my own heart wearies also for my home in England where those I love are keeping the feast this Christmas Eve. But we have work to do before we feast tonight. For this is Yuletide, and the heathen people of the forest have gathered at the Thunder-oak of Geismar to worship their god Thor. Strange things will be seen there, and deeds that make the soul black. But we are sent to lighten their darkness, and we will teach our kinsmen to keep a Christmas with us such as the woodland has never known. Forward, then, and let us stiffen up our feeble knees."

A murmur of assent came from the men. Even the horses seemed to take fresh heart. They flattened their backs to draw the heavy loads, and blew the frost from their nostrils as they pushed ahead.

The night grew broader and less oppressive. A gate of brightness was opened secretly somewhere in the sky; higher and higher swelled the clear flood of moonlight, until it poured over the eastern wall of forest into the road. A pack of wolves howled faintly in the distance, but they were receding, and the sound soon died away.

The stars sparkled merrily through the stringent air; the small, round moon shone like silver; little breaths of the dreaming wind wandered, whispering across the pointed fir-tops, as the pilgrims toiled bravely onward, following their clue of light through a labyrinth of darkness.

After a while the road began to open out a little. There were spaces of meadowland fringed with alders, behind which a boisterous river clashed through spears of ice.

Rude houses of hewn logs appeared in the openings, each one casting a patch of inky blackness on the snow. Then the travelers passed a larger group of dwellings, all silent and unlighted; and beyond, they saw a great house, with many outbuildings and enclosed courtyards, from which the hounds bayed furiously and a noise of stamping horses came from the stalls. But there was no other sound of life. The fields around lay bare to the moon. They saw no one, except once when, on a path that skirted the farther edge of a meadow, three dark figures ran by swiftly.

Then the road plunged again into a dense thicket, traversed it and, climbing to the left, emerged suddenly on a glade, round and level except at the northern side where a swelling hillock was crowned with a huge oak tree. It towered above the heath, a giant with contorted arms, beckoning to the host of lesser trees. "Here," cried Winfried, as his eyes flashed and his hand lifted his heavy staff, "here is the Thunder-oak; and here the cross of Christ shall break the hammer of the false god Thor."

III
IN THE SHADOW OF THE THUNDER-OAK

WITHERED LEAVES STILL CLUNG TO THE branches of the oak, torn and faded banners of the departed summer. The bright crimson of autumn had long since disappeared, bleached away by the storms and the cold. But tonight these tattered remnants of glory were red again, ancient bloodstains against the dark blue sky. For an immense fire had been kindled in front of the tree. Tongues of ruddy flame, fountains of ruby sparks, ascended through the spreading limbs and flung a fierce illumination upward and around. The pale, pure moonlight that bathed the surrounding forests was quenched and eclipsed here. Not a beam of it sifted downward through the branches of the oak. It stood like a pillar of cloud between the still sight of heaven and the crackling, flashing fire of earth.

But the fire itself was invisible to Winfried and his companions. Great throngs of people were gathered around it in a half circle, their backs to the open glade, their faces towards the oak. Seen against that glowing background, it was only the silhouette of a crowd, vague, black, formless, mysterious.

The travelers paused for a moment at the edge of the thicket and took counsel together.

"It is the assembly of the tribe," said one of the foresters, "the great night of the council. I heard of it three days ago as we passed through one of the villages. All who swear by the old gods have been summoned. They will sacrifice a steed to the god of war, and drink blood, and eat horseflesh to make them strong. It will be at the peril of our lives if we approach them. At least we must hide the cross if we want to escape death."

"Do not hide the cross," cried Winfried, lifting his staff, "for I have come to show it, and to make these blind folk see its power. There is more to be done here tonight than the slaying of a steed, and a greater evil to be stayed than the shameful eating of meat sacrificed to idols. I have seen it in a dream. Here the cross must stand and be our banner."

At his command the sled was left in the border of the wood, with two of the men to guard it, and the rest of the company moved forward across the open ground. They approached unnoticed, for all the multitude were looking intently towards the fire at the foot of the oak.

Then Winfried's voice rang out, "Hail, sons of the forest! A stranger claims the warmth of your fire in the winter night."

Swiftly, and as with a single motion, a thousand eyes were bent upon the speaker. The semicircle opened silently in the middle; Winfried entered with his followers; it closed again behind them.

Then, as they looked round the curving ranks, they saw that the color of the assemblage was not black, but white—dazzling, radiant, solemn. White, the robes of the women clustered together at the points of the wide crescent; white, the glittering chainmail of the warriors standing in close ranks; white, the fur mantles of the aged men who held the central place in the circle; white, with the shimmer of silver ornaments and the purity of lamb's wool, the garments of a little group of children who stood close by the fire; white, with awe and fear, the faces of all who looked at them; and over all the flickering, dancing radiance of the flames played and glimmered like a faint, vanishing tinge of blood on snow.

The only figure untouched by the glow was the old priest, Hunrad, with his long, spectral robe, flowing hair and beard, and dead-pale face, who stood with his back to the fire and advanced slowly to meet the strangers.

"Who are you? From where do you come, and what do you seek here?" His voice was as heavy and toneless as a muffled bell.

"I am your kinsman, of the German brother-hood," answered Winfried, "and from England, beyond the sea, I have come to bring you a greeting from that land, and a message from the All-Father, whose servant I am."

"Welcome, then," said Hunrad, "welcome, kinsman, and be silent; for what passes here is too high to wait, and must be done before the moon crosses the middle heaven, unless, indeed, you have some sign or token from the gods. Can you work miracles?"

The question came sharply, as if a sudden gleam of hope had flashed through the tangle of the old priest's mind. But Winfried's voice sank lower and a cloud of disappointment

passed over his face as he replied: "No, miracles have I never performed, though I have
heard of many; but the All-Father has given no
power to my hands above such as belongs to
common man."

"Stand still, then, you common man," said
Hunrad, scornfully, "and behold what the
gods have called us here to do. This night is
the death night of the sun god, Baldur the
Beautiful, beloved of gods and men. This
night is the hour of darkness and the power of
winter, of sacrifice and mighty fear. This night
the great Thor, the god of thunder and war,
to whom this oak is sacred, is grieved for the
death of Baldur, and angry with this people
because they have forsaken his worship. It is
long since an offering has been laid upon his
altar, long since the roots of his holy tree have
been fed with blood. Therefore its leaves have
withered before the time, and its boughs are
heavy with death. Therefore the Slavs and

the Wends have beaten us in battle. Therefore the harvests have failed, the wolf hordes have ravaged the sheepfolds, the strength has departed from the bow, the wood of the spear has broken, and the wild boar has slain the huntsman. Therefore the plague has fallen on our dwellings, and the dead are more than the living in all our villages. Answer me, my people, are not these things true?"

A hoarse sound of approval ran through the circle. A chant, in which the voices of the men and women blended, like the shrill wind in the pine trees above the rumbling thunder of a waterfall, rose and fell in rude cadences.

O Thor, the Thunderer,
Mighty and merciless,
Spare us from your blows!
Heave not your hammer,
Angry, against us;
Plague not your people.

Take from our treasure

The richest of ransom.

Silver we send you,

Jewels and javelins,

The best of garments.

All our possessions,

Priceless, we proffer.

Sheep we will slaughter,

Steeds we will sacrifice;

Bright blood shall bathe you,

O tree of Thunder;

Life floods shall cleanse you,

Strong wood of wonder.

Mighty one, have mercy,

Smite us no more,

Spare us and save us,

Spare us, Thor! Thor!

With two great shouts the song ended, and
a stillness followed, so intense that the crackling of the fire was heard distinctly. The old

priest stood silent for a moment. His shaggy brows swept down over his eyes like ashes quenching flame. Then he lifted his face and spoke.

"None of these things will please the god. More costly is the offering that shall cleanse your sin, more precious the crimson dew that shall send new life into this holy tree of blood. Thor claims your dearest and your noblest gift."

Hunrad moved nearer to the handful of children who stood watching the red mines in the fire and the swarms of spark serpents darting upward. They had heeded none of the priest's words, and did not notice now that he approached them, so eager were they to see which fiery snake would go highest among the oak branches. Foremost among them, and most intent on the pretty game, was a boy like a sunbeam, slender and quick, with blithe brown eyes and laughing lips. The priest's hand was laid upon his shoulder. The boy turned and looked up in his face.

"Here," said the old man, with his voice vibrating as when a thick rope is strained by a ship swinging from her moorings, "here is the chosen one, the eldest son of the chief, the dar-ling of the people. Hearken, Bernhard, will you go to Valhalla, where the heroes dwell with the gods, to bear a message to Thor?"

The boy answered, swift and clear: "Yes, priest, I will go if my father bids me. Is it far away? Shall I run quickly? Must I take my bow and arrows for the wolves?"

The boy's father, the chieftain Gundhar, stand-ing among his bearded warriors, drew his breath deep, and leaned so heavily on the handle of his spear that the wood cracked. And his wife, Irma, bending forward from the ranks of women, pushed the golden hair from her forehead with one hand while the other dragged at the silver chain about her neck until the rough links pierced her flesh and the red drops fell unheeded on the snow of her breast.

A sigh passed through the crowd, like the murmur of the forest before the storm breaks. Yet no one spoke but Hunrad:

"Yes, my Prince, both bow and spear you shall have, for the way is long, and you are a brave huntsman. But in darkness you must journey for a little space, and with eyes blindfolded. Are you afraid?"

"I fear nothing," said the boy, "neither darkness, nor the great bear, nor the werewolf. For I am Gundhar's son, and the defender of my people."

Then the priest led the child in his garment of lamb's wool to a broad stone in front of the fire. He gave him his little bow tipped with silver, and his spear with shining head of steel. He bound the child's eyes with a white cloth, and ordered him to kneel beside the stone with his face to the east. Unconsciously the wide arc of spectators drew inward toward the center, as the ends of the bow draw together when the cord is stretched. Winfried moved noiselessly until he stood close behind the priest.

The old man stooped to lift a black hammer of stone from the ground—the sacred hammer of the god Thor. Summoning all the strength of his withered arms, he swung it high in the air. It poised for an instant above the child's fair head— then turned to fall.

One keen cry shrilled out from where the women stood: "Me! Take me! Not Bernhard!"

The flight of the mother towards her child was as swift as the falcon's swoop. But swifter still was the hand of the deliverer.

Winfried's heavy staff thrust mightily against the hammer's handle as it fell. Sideways it glanced from the old man's grasp, and the black stone, striking on the altar's edge, split in two. A shout of awe and joy rolled along the living circle. The branches of the oak shivered. The flames leaped higher. As the shout died away, the people saw the lady Irma with her arms clasped round her child, and above them, on the altar stone, Winfried, his face shining like the face of an angel.

IV

THE FELLING OF THE TREE

IKE A SWIFT MOUNTAIN-FLOOD ROLLING DOWN its channel, a huge rock tumbling from the hillside and falling in mid-stream, and the baffled waters, broken and confused, pausing in their flow, dashing high against the rock, foaming and murmuring with divided impulse, uncertain whether to turn to the right or the left: even so Winfried's bold deed fell into the midst of the thoughts and passions of the council. They were at a standstill. Anger and wonder, reverence and joy and confusion surged through the crowd. They did not know which way to move: to resent the intrusion of the stranger as an insult to their gods, or to welcome him as the rescuer of their darling prince.

The old priest crouched by the altar, silent. Conflicting counsels troubled the air. Let the sacrifice go forward; the gods must be appeased. No, the boy must not die; bring the chieftain's best horse and slay it in his stead—it will be enough; the holy tree loves the blood of horses. Not so, there is a better counsel yet: seize the stranger whom the gods have led here as a victim and make his life pay the forfeit of his daring.

The withered leaves on the oak rustled and whispered overhead. The fire flared and sank again. The angry voices clashed against each other and fell like opposing waves. Then the chieftain Gundhar struck the earth with his spear and gave his decision.

"All have spoken, but none are agreed. There is no voice of the council. Keep silence now, and let the stranger speak. His words shall give us judgment, whether he is to live or to die."

Winfried lifted himself high upon the altar, drew a roll of parchment from his bosom, and began to read.

"A letter from the great Bishop of Rome, who sits on a golden throne, to the people of the forest, Hessians and Thuringians, Franks and Saxons. *In nomine Domini, sanctae et individuae trinitatis, amen!*"

A murmur of awe ran through the crowd. "It is the sacred tongue of the Romans, the tongue that is heard and understood by the wise men of every land. There is magic in it. Listen!"

Winfried went on to read the letter, translating it into the speech of the people.

"We have sent unto you our Brother Boniface, and appointed him your bishop, that he may teach you the only true faith, and baptize you and lead you back from the ways of error to the path of salvation. Hearken to him in all things like a father. Bow your hearts to his teaching. He does not come for earthly gain, but for the gain of your souls. Depart from evil works. Do not worship the false gods, for they are devils. Offer no more bloody sacrifices, nor eat the flesh of horses, but do as our Brother Boniface commands you. Build a house for him that he may dwell among you, and a church where you may offer your prayers to the only living God, the Almighty King of Heaven."

It was a splendid message, proud, strong, peaceful, loving. The dignity of the words imposed mightily upon the hearts of the people. They were quieted as those who have listened to a lofty strain of music.

"Tell us, then," said Gundhar, "what is the word that you bring to us from the Almighty. What is your counsel for the tribes of the wood-land on this night of sacrifice?"

"This is the word, and this is the counsel," answered Winfried. "Not a drop of blood shall fall tonight, except that which pity has drawn from the breast of your princess, in love for her child. Not a life shall be blotted out in the darkness tonight; but the great shadow of the tree that hides you from the light of heaven shall be swept away. For this is the birth night of the Christ, the Son of the All-Father and the Savior of mankind. He is fairer than Baldur the Beautiful, greater than Odin the Wise, kinder than Freya the Good. Since he has come to earth the bloody sacrifices must cease. The dark Thor, on whom you vainly call, is dead. Deep in the shades of Niffelheim he is lost forever. His power in the world is broken. Will you serve a helpless god? See, my brothers, you call this tree his oak. Does he dwell here? Does he protect it?"

A troubled voice of assent rose from the throng. The people stirred uneasily. Women covered their eyes. Hunrad lifted his head and muttered hoarsely, "Thor! Take vengeance! Thor!"

Winfried beckoned to Gregor. "Bring the axes, yours and one for me. Now, young woodsman, show your craft! The king-tree of the forest must fall, and swiftly, or all is lost!"

The two men took their places facing each other, one on each side of the oak. Their cloaks were flung aside, their heads bare. Carefully they felt the ground with their feet, seeking a firm grip on the earth. Firmly they grasped the axe handles and swung the shining blades.

"Tree-god!" cried Winfried, "Are you angry? This is how we smite you!"

"Tree-god!" answered Gregor, "Are you mighty? This is how we fight you!"

Clang! Clang! The alternate strokes beat time upon the hard, ringing wood. The axe-heads glittered in their rhythmic flight, like fierce eagles circling about their quarry.

The broad flakes of wood flew from the deepening gashes in the sides of the oak. The huge trunk quivered. There was a shuddering in the branches. Then the great wonder of Winfried's life came to pass.

Out of the stillness of the winter night, a mighty rushing noise sounded overhead.

Was it the ancient gods on their white battle-steeds, with their black hounds of wrath and their arrows of lightning, sweeping through the air to destroy their foes?

A strong, whirling wind passed over the tree-tops. It gripped the oak by its branches and tore it from its roots. Backward it fell, like a ruined tower, groaning and crashing as it split into four great pieces.

Winfried let his axe drop and bowed his head for a moment in the presence of almighty power.

Then he turned to the people, "Here is the timber," he cried, "already felled and split for your new building. On this spot shall rise a chapel to the true God and his servant Saint Peter.

"And here," he said, as his eyes fell on a young fir tree, standing straight and green, with its top pointing towards the stars, amid the divided ruins of the fallen oak, "here is the living tree, with no stain of blood upon it, that shall be the sign of your new worship. See how it points to the sky. Let us call it the tree of the Christ-child. Take it up and carry it to the chieftain's hall. You shall go no more into the shadows of the forest to keep your feasts with secret rites of shame. You shall keep them at home, with laughter and song and rites of love. The Thunder-oak has fallen, and I think the day is coming when there shall not be a home in all Germany where the children are not gathered around the green fir-tree to rejoice in the birth night of Christ."

So they took the little fir from its place, carried it in joyous procession to the edge of the glade, and laid it on the sled. The horses tossed their heads and drew their load bravely, as if the new burden had made it lighter.

When they came to the house of Gundhar, he ordered them to throw open the doors of the hall and set the tree in the midst of it. They kindled lights among the branches until it seemed to be tangled full of fireflies. The children encircled it, wondering, and the sweet odor of the balsam filled the house.

Then Winfried stood beside the chair of Gundhar, on the dais at the end of the hall, and told the story of Bethlehem, of the babe in the manger, of the shepherds on the hills, of the host of angels and their midnight song. All the people listened, charmed into stillness.

But the boy Bernhard, on Irma's knee, folded by her soft arm, grew restless as the story lengthened and began to prattle softly at his mother's ear.

"Mother," whispered the child, "why did you cry out so loud, when the priest was going to send me to Valhalla?"

"Oh, hush, my child," answered the mother, and pressed him closer to her side.

"Mother," whispered the boy again, laying his finger on the stains upon her breast, "see, your dress is red! What are these stains? Did someone hurt you?"

The mother closed his mouth with a kiss. "Dear, be still, and listen!"

The boy obeyed. His eyes were heavy with sleep. But he heard the last words of Winfried as he spoke of the angelic messengers flying over the hills of Judea and singing as they flew. The child wondered and dreamed and listened. Suddenly his face grew bright. He put his lips close to Irma's cheek again.

"Oh, mother!" he whispered very low, "Do not speak. Do you hear them? Those angels have come back again. They are singing now behind the tree."

And some say that it was true; but others say that it was only Gregor and his companions at the lower end of the hall, chanting their Christmas hymn:

> All glory be to God on high,
> And to the earth be peace!
> Good will, henceforth, from heaven
>   to man
> Begin, and never cease.

the Christmas Angel

I T WAS THE HOUR OF REST IN THE COUNTRY
beyond the stars. All the silver bells that
swing with the turning of the great ring of light
that lies around that land were softly chiming,
and the sound of their commotion went down
like dew upon the golden ways of the city, the
long alleys of blossoming trees, the meadows of
asphodel, and the curving shores of the River of
Life.

At the hearing of that chime, all the angels who had been working turned to play, and all who had been playing gave themselves joyfully to work. Those who had been singing and making melody on different instruments fell silent and began to listen. Those who had been walking alone in meditation met together in companies to talk. And those who had been far away on errands to the Earth and other planets came homeward like a flight of swallows to the high cliff when the day is over.

It was not that they needed to be restored from weariness, for the inhabitants of that country never say, "I am tired." But there, as here, the law of change is the secret of happiness, and the joy that never ends is woven of mingled strands of labor and repose, society and solitude, music and silence. Sleep comes to them not as it does to us, with a darkening of the vision and a folding of the wings of the spirit, but with an opening of the eyes to deeper and fuller light, and with an effortless outgoing of the soul upon broader currents of life, as the sun-loving bird poises and circles upward, without a wing beat, on the upholding air.

It was in one of the quiet corners of the green valley called Peacefield, where the little brook of Brighthopes runs smoothly down to join the River of Life, that I saw a company of angels, returned from various labors on Earth, sitting in friendly conversation on the hillside, where cyclamens and arbutus and violets and fringed orchids and pale lady's-tresses, and all the sweet-smelling flowers that are separated in the lower world by the seasons, were thrown together in a harmony of fragrance. There were three of the company who seemed to be leaders, distinguished not only by more radiant and powerful looks, but by a tone of authority in their speech and by the willing attention with which the others listened to them as they talked of their earthly tasks, of the tangles and troubles, the wars and miseries that they had seen among mankind, and the best way to get rid of them and bring sorrow to an end.

"The Earth is full of oppression and unrighteousness," said the tallest and most powerful of the angels. His voice was deep and strong, and by his shining armor and the long two-handed sword hanging over his shoulder I knew that he was the archangel Michael, the mightiest one among the warriors of the King and the executor of the divine judgments upon the unjust. "The Earth is tormented with injustice," he cried, "and the great misery that I have seen among mankind is that the evil hand is often stronger than the good hand and can beat it down.

"The arm of the cruel is heavier than the arm of the kind. The unjust get the better of the just and tread on them. I have seen tyrant kings crush their helpless folk. I have seen the fields of the innocent trampled into bloody ruin by the feet of conquering armies. I have seen wicked nations overcome peoples that loved liberty and take away their treasure by force of arms. I have seen poverty mocked by arrogant wealth, and purity deflowered by brute violence, and gentleness and fair dealing bruised in the winepress of iniquity and pride.

"There is no cure for this evil, but by the giving of greater force to the good hand. The righteous cause must be strengthened with might to resist the wicked, to defend the helpless, to punish all cruelty and unfairness, to uphold the right everywhere, and to enforce justice with unconquerable arms. Oh, that the host of heaven might be called, arrayed, and sent to mingle in the wars of mankind, to make the good victorious, to destroy all evil, and to make the will of the King prevail!

"We would shake down the thrones of tyrants, and loose the bands of the oppressed. We would hold the cruel and violent with the bit of fear, and drive the greedy and fierce-minded with the whip of terror. We would stand guard, with weapons drawn, about the innocent, the gentle, and the kind, and keep the peace of God with the sword of the angels!"

As he spoke, his hands were lifted to the hilt of his long blade, and he raised it above him, straight and shining, throwing sparkles of light around it, like the spray from the sharp prow of a moving ship. Bright flames of heavenly ardor leaped in the eyes of the listening angels; a martial air passed over their faces as if they longed for the call to war.

But no silver trumpet blared from the battlements of the City of God; no crimson flag was unfurled on those high, secret walls; no thrilling drumbeat echoed over the smooth meadow. Only the sound of the brook of Brighthopes was heard tinkling and murmuring among the roots of the grasses and flowers; and far off a cadence of song drifted down from the inner courts of the Palace of the King.

Then another angel began to speak, and he made answer to Michael. He, too, was tall and wore the look of power. But it was power of the mind rather than of the hand. His face was clear and glistening, and his eyes were lit with a steady flame that neither leaped nor fell. Of flame also were his garments, which clung about him as the fire enwraps a burning torch where there is no wind; and his great wings, soaring to a point far above his head, were like a living lamp before the altar of the Most High. By this sign I knew that it was the archangel Uriel, the spirit of the sun, clearest in vision, deepest in wisdom of all the spirits that surround the throne.

"I hold not the same thought," he said, "as the great archangel Michael; nor, though I desire the same end that he desires, would I seek it by the same way. For I know how often power has been given to the good, and how often it has been turned aside and used for evil. I know that the host of heaven and the very stars in their courses have fought on the side of a favored nation; yet pride has followed triumph, and oppression has been the firstborn child of victory. I know that the deliverers of the people have become tyrants over those whom they have set free, and the fighters for liberty have been changed into the soldiers of fortune. Power corrupts itself, and might cannot save.

"Does not the Prince Michael remember how the angel of the Lord led the armies of Israel, and gave them the battle against every foe except the enemy within the camp? And how they robbed and crushed the peoples against whom they had fought for freedom? And how the wickedness of the tribes of Canaan survived their conquest and overcame their conquerors, so that the children of Israel learned to worship the idols of their enemies, Moloch, Baal, and Ashtoreth?

"Power corrupts itself, and might cannot save. Was not Persia the destroyer of Babylon, and did not the tyranny of Persia cry aloud for destruction? Did not Rome break the yoke of the East, and does not the yoke of Rome lie heavy on the shoulders of the world? Listen!"

There was silence for a moment on the slopes of Peacefield, and then over the encircling hills a cool wind brought the sound of chains clanking in prisons and galleys, the sighing of millions of slaves, the weeping of wretched women and children, the blows of hammers nailing men to their crosses. Then the sound passed by with the wind, and Uriel spoke again:

"Power corrupts itself, and might cannot save. The Earth is full of ignorant strife, and for this evil there is no cure but by the giving of greater knowledge. It is because men do not understand evil that they yield themselves to its power. Wickedness is folly in action, and injustice is the error of the blind. It is because men are ignorant that they destroy one another, and at last themselves.

"If there were more light in the world there would be no sorrow. If the great King who knows all things would enlighten the world with wisdom—wisdom to understand his law and his ways, to read the secrets of the earth and the stars, to discern the workings of the heart of man and the things that make for joy and peace—if he would but send us, his messengers, as a flame of fire to shine upon those who sit in darkness, how gladly would we go to bring in the new day!

"We would speak the word of warning and counsel to the erring, and tell knowledge to the perplexed. We would guide the ignorant in the paths of prudence, and the young would sit at our feet and hear us gladly in the school of life. Then folly would fade away as the morning vapor, and the sun of wisdom would shine on all mankind, and the peace of God would come with the counsel of the angels."

A murmur of pleasure followed the words of Uriel, and eager looks flashed around the circle of the messengers of light as they heard the praise of wisdom fitly spoken. But there was one among them on whose face a shadow of doubt rested, and though he smiled, it was as if he remembered something that the others had forgotten.

He turned to an angel near him.

"Who was it," said he, "to whom you were sent with counsel long ago? Was it not Balaam, the son of Beor, as he was riding to meet the king of Moab? And did not even the dumb beast profit more by your instruction than the man who rode him? And who was it," he continued, turning to Uriel, "that was called the wisest of all humans, having searched out and understood the many inventions that are found under the sun? Was not Solomon, prince of fools and philosophers, unable by much learning to escape weariness of the flesh and despair of the spirit? Knowledge also is vanity and vexation. This I know well, because I have dwelt among humans and held converse with them since the day when I was sent to instruct the first man in Eden."

Then I looked more closely at the one who was speaking and recognized the beauty of the archangel Raphael, as it was pictured long ago:

A seraph winged; six wings he wore to shade
His lineaments divine; the pair that clad
Each shoulder broad came mantling o'er
    his breast,
With regal ornament; the middle pair
Girt like a starry zone his waist, and round
Skirted his loins and thighs with downy gold
And colors dipped in heav'n; the third his feet
Shadowed from either heel with feathered mail,
Sky-tinctured grain. Like Maia's son he stood
And shook his plumes, so that heavenly
    fragrance filled
The circuit wide.

"Too well I know," he spoke on, while the smile on his face deepened into a look of pity and tenderness and desire, "too well I know that power corrupts itself and that knowledge cannot save. There is no cure for the evil in the world but by the giving of more love to mortals. The laws that are ordained for Earth are strange and unequal, and the ways where mankind must walk are full of pitfalls and dangers. Pestilence creeps along the ground and flows in the rivers; whirlwind and tempest shake the habitations of mankind and drive their ships to destruction; fire breaks forth from the mountains, and the foundations of the world tremble. Frail is the flesh of mortals, and many are their pains and troubles. Their children can never find peace until the children learn to love one another and to help one another.

"Wickedness is begotten by disease and misery. Violence comes from poverty and hunger. The cruelty of oppression is when the strong tread the weak under their feet; the bitterness

71

of pride is when the wise and learned despise the simple; the crown of folly is when the rich think they are gods, and the poor think there is no God.

"Hatred and envy and contempt are the curse of life. And for these there is no remedy but love—the will to give and to bless—the will of the King himself, who gives to all and is loving unto every person. But how shall the hearts of men be won to this will? How shall it enter into them and possess them? Even the gods that humans fashion for themselves are cruel and proud and false and unjust. How shall the miracle be wrought in human nature to reveal the meaning of humanity? How shall mortals be made like God?"

At this question a deep hush fell around the circle, and every listener was still, even as the rustling leaves hang motionless when the light breeze falls away in the hour of sunset. Then through the silence, like the song of a faraway thrush from its hermitage in the forest, a voice came ringing: "I know, I know, I know how."

Clear and sweet—clear as a ray of light, sweeter than the smallest silver bell that rings the hour of rest—was that slender voice floating on the odorous and translucent air. Nearer and nearer it came, echoing down the valley, "I know, I know, I know how!"

Then from between the rounded hills, among which the brook of Brighthopes is born, appeared a young angel, a little child with flying hair of gold and green wreaths twined about his shoulders, and fluttering hands that played upon the air and seemed to lift him so lightly that he had no need of wings. As thistledown blown by the wind dances across the water, so he came along the little stream, singing clear above the murmur of the brook.

All the angels rose and turned to look at him with wondering eyes. Multitudes of others came flying swiftly to the place from which the strange, new song was sounding. Rank upon rank, like a garden of living flowers, they stood along the sloping banks of the brook while the child-angel floated into the midst of them, singing: "I know, I know, I know how! Humans shall be made like God because the Son of God shall become a human."

At this all the angels looked at one another with amazement, and gathered more closely about the child-angel, as those who hear wonderful news.

"How can this be?" they asked. "How is it possible that the Son of God should be a human?"

"I do not know," said the young angel. "I only know that it is to be."

"But if he becomes a human," said Raphael, "he will be at the mercy of humans; the cruel and the wicked will have power upon him; he will suffer."

"I know it," answered the young angel, "and by suffering he will understand the meaning of all sorrow and pain; he will be able to comfort everyone who weeps; his own tears will be for the healing of sad hearts; and those who are healed by him will learn for his sake to be kind to each other."

"But if the Son of God is a true human," said Uriel, "he must first be a child, simple, and lowly, and helpless. It may be that he will never gain the learning of the schools. The masters of earthly wisdom will despise him and speak scorn of him."

"I know it," said the young angel, "but in meekness he will answer them; and to those who become as little children he will give the heavenly wisdom that comes, without seeking, to the pure and gentle of heart."

"But if he becomes a human," said Michael, "evil humans will hate and persecute him: They may even take his life, if they are stronger than he."

"I know it," answered the young angel. "They will nail him to a cross. But when he is lifted up, he will draw all mankind unto him, for he will still be the Son of God, and no heart that is open to love can help loving him, since his love for mortals is so great that he is willing to die for them."

"But how do you know these things?" cried the other angels. "Who are you?"

"I am the Christmas angel," he said. "At first I was sent as the dream of a little child, a holy child, blessed and wonderful, to dwell in the heart of a pure virgin, Mary of Nazareth. There I was hidden till the word came to call me back to the throne of the King, and tell me my name, and give me my new message. For this is Christmas day on Earth, and today the Son of God is born of a woman. So I must fly quickly, before the sun rises, to bring the good news to those happy mortals who have been chosen to receive them."

As he said this, the young angel rose, with arms outspread, from the green meadow of Peacefield and, passing over the bounds of Heaven, dropped swiftly as a shooting star toward the night shadow of the Earth. The other angels followed him—a throng of dazzling forms, beautiful as a rain of jewels falling from the dark-blue sky. But the child-angel went more swiftly than the others, because of the certainty of gladness in his heart.

And as the others followed him they wondered who had been favored and chosen to receive the glad tidings.

"It must be the emperor of the world and his counselors," they thought. But the flight passed over Rome.

"It may be the philosophers and the masters of learning," they thought. But the flight passed over Athens.

"Can it be the high priest of the Jews, and the elders and the scribes?" they thought. But the flight passed over Jerusalem.

It floated out over the hill country of Bethlehem, the throng of silent angels holding close together as if perplexed and doubtful. The child-angel darted on far in advance, as one who knows the way through the darkness.

The villages were all still: the very houses seemed asleep. But in one place there was a low sound of talking in a stable, near an inn—a sound as of a mother soothing her baby to rest.

All over the pastures on the hillsides a light film of snow had fallen, delicate as the veil of a bride adorned for her marriage; and as the child-angel passed over them, alone in the swiftness of his flight, the pure fields sparkled around him, giving back his radiance.

And in that region there were shepherds out in the field, keeping watch over their flock by night. And an angel of the Lord appeared to them, and the glory of the Lord shone around them, and they were filled with fear.

And the angel said to them, "Be not afraid; for behold, I bring you good news of a great joy which will come to all the people; for to you is born this day in the city of David a Savior, who is Christ the Lord. And this will be a sign for you: you will find a babe wrapped in swaddling cloths and lying in a manger."

And suddenly there was with the angel a multitude of the heavenly host praising God and saying, "Glory to God in the highest, and on earth peace among men with whom he is pleased!"

When the angels went away from them into heaven, the shepherds said to one another, "Let us go over to Bethlehem and see this thing that has happened, which the Lord has made known to us."

So I said within myself that I also would go with the shepherds, even to Bethlehem. And I heard a great and sweet voice, as of a bell, that said, "Come!" And when the bell had sounded twelve times, I awoke; and it was Christmas morn; and I knew that I had been in a dream.

Yet it seemed to me that the things that I had heard were true.

Christmas-Giving
and
Christmas-Living

THE CUSTOM OF EXCHANGING PRESENTS ON A certain day in the year is very much older than Christmas, and means very much less. It has been observed in almost all ages of the world and among many different nations. It is a fine thing or a foolish thing, as the case may be; an encouragement to friendliness, or a tribute to fashion; an expression of good nature, or a bid for favor; an outgoing of generosity, or a disguise of greed; a cheerful old custom, or a futile old farce, according to the spirit that animates it and the form it takes.

But when this ancient and variously inter-preted tradition of a day of gifts was transferred to the Christmas season, it was brought into vital contact with an idea that would transform it, and with an example that must lift it up to a higher plane. The example is the life of Jesus. The idea is unselfish interest in the happiness of others.

The great gift of Jesus to the world was himself. He lived with and for men and women. He kept back nothing. In every particular and personal gift that he made to certain people there was something of himself that made it precious.

For example, at the wedding in Cana of Galilee, it was his thought for the feelings of the giver of the feast and his wish that every guest should find due entertainment that lent the flavor of a heavenly hospitality to the wine that he provided.

When he gave bread and fish to the hungry multitude that had followed him out among the hills by the Lake of Gennesaret, the people were refreshed and strengthened by the sense of Jesus' personal care for their welfare as much as by the food that he bestowed upon them. It was another illustration of the sweetness of "a dinner of herbs, where love is."

The gifts of healing that he conferred upon many different kinds of sufferers were, in every case, evidences that Jesus was willing to give something of himself, his thought, his sympathy, his vital power, to the men and women among whom he lived. Once, when a paralytic was brought to Jesus on a bed, he surprised everybody, and offended many, by giving the poor wretch the pardon of his sins before he gave new life to his body. That was just because Jesus thought before he gave, because he desired to satisfy the deepest need, because in fact he gave something of himself in every gift. All true Christmas-giving ought to be after this pattern.

Not that it must all be solemn and serious. For the most part it deals with little wants, little joys, little tokens of friendly feeling. But the feeling must be more than the token; otherwise the gift does not really belong to Christmas.

It takes time and effort and unselfish expenditure of strength to make gifts in this way. But it is the only way that fits the season.

The finest Christmas gift is not the one that costs the most money, but the one that carries the most love.

II

BUT HOW SELDOM CHRISTMAS COMES—ONLY ONCE a year; and how soon it is over—a night and a day! If that is the whole of it, it seems not much more durable than the little toys that one buys on the street-corner. They run for an hour, and then the spring breaks and the legs come off, and nothing remains but a contribution to the garbage bin.

But surely that need not and ought not to be the whole of Christmas—only a single day of generosity, ransomed from the dull servitude of a selfish year; only a single night of merry-making, celebrated in the slave-quarters of a selfish race! If every gift is the token of a personal thought, a friendly feeling, an unselfish interest in the joy of others, then the thought, the feeling, the interest, may remain after the gift is made.

The little present or the rare and long-wished-for gift (no matter whether the vessel is of gold, or silver, or iron, or wood, or clay, or just a small bit of birch bark folded into a cup) may carry a message something like this:

"I am thinking of you today, because it is Christmas, and I wish you happiness. And tomorrow, because it will be the day after Christmas, I will still wish you happiness; and so on, clear through the year. I may not be able to tell you about it every day, because I may be far away, or because both of us may be very busy, or perhaps because I cannot even afford to pay the postage on so many letters or find the time to write them. But that makes no difference. The thought and the wish will be here just the same. In my work and in the business of life I mean to try not to be unfair to you or to injure you in any way. In my pleasure, if we can be together, I would like to share the fun with you. Whatever joy or success comes to you will make me glad. Without pretense, and in plain words, good will to you is what I mean, in the Spirit of Christmas."

It is not necessary to put a message like this into high-flown language, such as swearing absolute devotion and deathless consecration. In love and friendship, small, steady payments on a cash basis are better than immense promissory notes. Nor, indeed, is it always necessary to put the message into words at all, nor even to convey it by a tangible token. To feel it and to act it out— that is the main thing.

There are a great many people in the world whom we know more or less but to whom for various reasons we cannot very well send a Christmas gift. But there is hardly one in all the circles of our acquaintance with whom we may not exchange the touch of Christmas life.

In the outer circles, cheerful greetings, courtesy, consideration; in the inner circles, sympathetic interest, hearty congratulations, honest encouragement; in the inmost circle, comradeship, helpfulness, tenderness—

"Beautiful friendship, tried by sun and wind,
Durable from the daily dust of life."

After all, Christmas-living is the best kind of Christmas-giving.

Christmas Prayers

A CHRISTMAS PRAYER FOR THE HOME

Father of all mankind, look upon our family,
Kneeling together before you,
And grant us a true Christmas.

With loving heart we bless you:
For the gift of your dear Son Jesus Christ,
For the peace he brings to our homes,

For the goodwill he teaches to sinful
mankind,
For the glory of your goodness shining
in his face.

With joyful voice we praise you:
For his lowly birth and his resting in the
manger,
For the pure tenderness of his mother Mary,
For the fatherly care that protected him,
For the Providence that saved the holy Child
To be the Savior of the world.

With deep desire we beseech you:
Help us to keep his birthday truly,
Help us to offer, in his name, our
Christmas prayer.

From the sickness of sin and the darkness
of doubt,

From selfish pleasures and sullen pains,

From the frost of pride and the fever of envy,

    God save us every one, through the blessing

    of Jesus.

In the health of purity and the calm of

mutual trust,

In the sharing of joy and the bearing of trouble,

In the steady glow of love and the clear light

    of hope,

God keep us every one, by the blessing of Jesus.

In praying and praising, in giving and receiving,

In eating and drinking, in singing and

    making merry,

In parents' gladness and in children's mirth,

In dear memories of those who have departed,

In good comradeship with those who are here,

In kind wishes for those who are far away,

In patient waiting, sweet contentment,
generous cheer,
God bless us every one, with the blessing of
Jesus.

By remembering our kinship with all mankind,
By well-wishing, friendly speaking and kindly
doing,
By cheering the downcast and adding sunshine
to daylight,
By welcoming strangers
(poor shepherds or wise men),
By keeping the music of the angels' song in
this home,
God help us every one to share the blessing
of Jesus:
In whose name we keep Christmas,
And in whose words we pray together:

Our Father who art in heaven, hallowed be
thy name.
Thy kingdom come. Thy will be done in earth,
as it is in heaven.
Give us this day our daily bread. And forgive
us our debts, as we forgive our debtors.
And lead us not into temptation, but deliver
us from evil:
For thine is the kingdom, and the power, and
the glory, forever and ever.
Amen.

A CHRISTMAS PRAYER FOR
THE LONELY FOLKS

Lord God of the solitary,

Look upon me in my loneliness.

Since I may not keep this Christmas in the home,

Send it into my heart.

Do not let my sins cloud me in,

But shine through them with forgiveness

   in the face of the child Jesus.

Put me in loving remembrance of the lowly
　　lodging in the stable of Bethlehem,
The sorrows of the blessed Mary, the poverty
　　and exile of the Prince of Peace.
For his sake, give me cheerful courage to
　　endure my lot,
And inward comfort to sweeten it.

Purge my heart from hard and bitter
　　　　thoughts.
Let no shadow of forgetting come between me
　　and friends far away;
Bless them in their Christmas mirth.
Hedge me in with faithfulness,
That I may not grow unworthy to meet
　　them again.

Give me good work to do,
So that I may forget myself and find peace in
　　doing it for you.

Though I am poor, send me to carry some gift
    to those who are poorer,
Some cheer to those who are lonelier.
Grant me the joy to do a kindness to one of
    your little ones:
Light my Christmas candle at the gladness of
    an innocent and grateful heart.

Strange is the path where you lead me:
Let me not doubt your wisdom, nor lose your
    hand.
Make me sure that Eternal Love is revealed
    in Jesus, your dear Son,
To save us from sin and solitude and death.
Teach me that I am not alone,
But that many hearts all around the world
Join with me through the silence while I pray
    in his name:

Our Father who art in heaven, hallowed be
    thy name.

*Thy kingdom come. Thy will be done in earth,
  as it is in heaven.*

*Give us this day our daily bread. And forgive us
  our debts, as we forgive our debtors.*

*And lead us not into temptation, but deliver us
  from evil:*

*For thine is the kingdom, and the power, and the
  glory, forever and ever.*

Amen.

Who We Are

Paraclete Press is a publisher of books, recordings, and DVDs on Christian spirituality. Our publishing represents a full expression of Christian belief and practice—from Catholic to Evangelical, from Protestant to Orthodox.

We are the publishing arm of the Community of Jesus, an ecumenical monastic community in the Benedictine tradition. As such, we are uniquely positioned in the marketplace without connection to a large corporation and with informal relationships to many branches and denominations of faith.

What We Are Doing

Books

Paraclete publishes books that show the richness and depth of what it means to be Christian. Although Benedictine spirituality is at the heart of all that we do, we publish books that reflect the Christian experience across many cultures, time periods, and houses of worship. We publish books that nourish the vibrant life of the church and its people—books about spiritual practice, formation, history, ideas, and customs.

We have several different series, including the best-selling Paraclete Essentials and Paraclete Giants series of classic texts in contemporary English; A Voice from the Monastery—men and women monastics writing about living a spiritual life today; award-winning literary faith fiction and poetry; and the Active Prayer Series that brings creativity and liveliness to any life of prayer.

Recordings

From Gregorian chant to contemporary American choral works, our music recordings celebrate sacred choral music through the centuries. Paraclete distributes the recordings of the internationally acclaimed choir Gloriæ Dei Cantores, praised for their "rapt and fathomless spiritual intensity" by *American Record Guide,* and the Gloriæ Dei Cantores Schola, which specializes in the study and performance of Gregorian chant. Paraclete is also the exclusive North American distributor of the recordings of the Monastic Choir of St. Peter's Abbey in Solesmes, France, long considered to be a leading authority on Gregorian chant.

DVDs

Our DVDs offer spiritual help, healing, and biblical guidance for life issues: grief and loss, marriage, forgiveness, anger management, facing death, and spiritual formation.

Learn more about us at our website:
www.paracletepress.com, or call us toll-free
at 1-800-451-5006.

YOU MAY ALSO BE INTERESTED IN . . .

O Christmas Three

by
O. Henry,
Tolstoy,
and Dickens

$16.99 Hardcover
ISBN 978-1-55725-776-5

This beautiful gift book contains three heartwarming stories that recall Christmases past:

O. HENRY'S all-American tale "The Gift of the Magi," originally published in 1906.

LEO TOLSTOY'S Russian folktale "Where Love Is, There God Is Also," from 1887.

CHARLES DICKENS'S little-known classic "What Christmas Is, As We Grow Older," from 1851.

The Story of the Other Wise Man

by Henry van Dyke

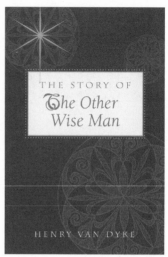

$14.95 Hardcover
ISBN: 978-1-55725-610-2

ONE OF THE MOST MEANINGFUL STORIES EVER WRITTEN...

"You know the story of the Three Wise Men of the East, and how they traveled from far away to offer their gifts at the manger-cradle in Bethlehem. But have you ever heard the story of the Other Wise Man?"

So begins Henry van Dyke's Christmas classic, told in the manner of the great fairy tales—and like a great fairy tale, it couldn't be more true! This beautiful edition is designed so that you can read *The Other Wise Man* as it is intended to be read—slowly.

Available from most booksellers or through Paraclete Press:
www.paracletepress.com; 1-800-451-5006.
Try your local bookstore first.